Native American Zodiac and Spirit Animals

written by JS Moore
illustrated by Janka Latečková

Understanding Apples Press
Kingsport, Tennessee

Native American Zodiac and Spirit Animals

JS Moore

1012 Whippoorwill Lane

Kingsport, TN 37660

http://www.understandingapples.com

ISBN-13 **ISBN:** 9798862885736

Printed in the United States of America

Preface

As you read this guidebook, take note of the similarities between Native American astrology and Western astrology. What makes the Native American system different, however, is that its symbols are very concrete and grounded. They can be found in our everyday environment and everywhere in nature.

Every single personality trait embodied by the spirit animals are attributes directly taken from the Native Americans' individual experiences with nature. If one truly examines their strengths and weaknesses, every animal is positive and negative in their own way.

This can seem overly complex at first, but the interplay of this duality reveals just how beautiful and diverse nature can be, especially as the canvas comes to life through the original watercolors of Janka Lateckova. As we unpack this unparalleled beauty, we discover an understanding of the sacred realm of astrology and what I will call a universal order to things both seen and unseen.

Carry this sacred knowledge with you wherever you may go, share it with others along your path, and use this guidebook to find your place on this beautiful earth!

Examining the Medicine Wheel closely, please realize that, like time itself, it is always in motion. Also, like Eastern philosophy and the *yin and yang* symbol, the Medicine Wheel depicts each season. The Celtic Cross is no different.

<u>Autumn</u>

Black (sometimes shown as green) represents Autumn. Black is also ascribed to the direction West. Autumn reminds us to prepare for winter and to look closely into the darker spaces.

Here we find the Snake has shed its skin in anticipation of change. We also find the diligent Beaver working tirelessly as the sun is setting low in the sky.

Winter

White represents Winter. White is also ascribed to the direction North. Winter is a time of deep reflection and healing. It is also the season of wisdom and vivid dreams.

Here we find the Bear rejuvenating and the White Bison in full protection mode overseeing the herd.

Spring

Yellow represents Spring. Yellow is also ascribed to the direction East. Spring is the season of the rising sun and the cacophony of sounds as all animals are active and reproducing.

Here we find the Falcon circling in the sky and the Owl both guarding the nest and bringing food for the young.

Summer

Red represents Summer. Red is also ascribed to the direction South. Summer is the season of the sun in its full glory, a vivid and blinding array. The animals are growing into adulthood, maturing.

Here, the Wolf stands proudly atop the mountain with the support of its pack.

TABLE OF CONTENTS

Otter (Aquarius) 08
Wolf (Pisces) 10
Falcon (Aries) 12
Beaver (Taurus) 14
Deer (Gemini) 16
Woodpecker (Cancer) 18
Salmon (Leo) 20
Brown Bear (Virgo) 22
Raven (Libra) 24
Snake (Scorpio) 26
Owl (Sagittarius) 28
Goose (Capricorn) 30

Otter

January 20 – February 18
Alternate Zodiac Sign: Aquarius
Element: Air

The Otter is a breaker of norms and quite often distinguishes itself from the crowd. As an Otter, you may find yourself habitually questioning the beliefs other people might have on all kinds of issues.

This natural capacity and desire to question everything naturally helps you in your creative pursuits. Traditions do not limit you, and you will often find a way to completely outdo or surpass any convention.

Indeed, you are as free as your standards, and this is reflected in the way you handle friendships and relationships. You are loyal only to those you have sworn to help. The numbers may be few, but your devotion to the people around you is limitless.

Consistent with your desire to stand out, you will often display your affection in ways that might seem out of the ordinary. Outsiders may sometimes criticize you for being over-the-top, but your loved ones respect you for who you are.

You are also fiercely loyal. Anyone who befriends you can rest in the knowledge that your love for them is true and genuine.

Wolf

February 19 – March 20
Alternate Zodiac Sign: Pisces
Element: Air and Water

The Wolf is a creature that does not think of itself alone, but the safety of the pack. They are treated as amplifiers in their immediate vicinity, increasing the emotional intensity already present around them.

At work, this means that if your team is mad, then you might just add to the flame by being angry yourself. However, it also works in a positive sense: if the energy in the room is positive, you will likewise bounce that energy around, keeping everyone happy.

You are an emotional creature – sensitive to the needs of others and will likewise respond to everything around you with alacrity. If a friend is in need, you are the first to try and make them feel comfortable.

You are also proud and incapable of tolerating any disrespectful act from other people. Once you are riled up, the beast within you can truly awaken and hurt others. In your righteous rage, you may end up accidentally turning on your friends.

Thus, your goal in life is to learn how to truly master your emotions.

Falcon

March 21 – April 19
Alternate Zodiac Sign: Aries
Element: Fire

In Native American zodiac, the Falcon is a true
force of nature. Imperious, fearless, and

brimming with charisma and leadership, many who possess this sign are known for being bringers of order and strength.

On an individual level, they can view any situation objectively and set aside their own prejudices. As such, being a Falcon allows you to function at the worst possible moments. No matter how stressful a situation is, you never give up self-control.

In terms of relationships, they are courageous and will often take the first step. They are trend-setters capable of dictating where a relationship or partnership is going to go, and it all boils down to their desire to always achieve first.

At times, they can be annoyingly self-assured, but that is only because the Falcon has great confidence – like you. You should nevertheless listen once your pride starts to bother other people as it could be problematic later.

Beaver

April 20 – May 20
Alternate Zodiac Sign: Taurus
Element: Fire and Air

The Beaver is another crucial animal in the
Native American Zodiac. As a sign, it signifies

materialism and individual ingenuity. This means that as a rule, you value being able to live materially and comfortably.

Some may have their qualms about your materialistic lifestyle, but contrary to what people might think, it is not because you think meaning lies in possessions alone.
It is because you know that for you and your loved ones to live properly, you need to work for a few things. Consequently, this means you are industrious and full of wit: always clever in finding ways to squeeze some extra income into your wallet.

However, you can also be unnecessarily jealous. Since you have established your life's standards from the material world, you are always concerned about how much your friends earn.

This draws out the competitor within you, causing certain rifts with people. This may also cause you to burn bridges in the most extreme cases.

Deer

May 21 – June 20
Alternate Zodiac Sign: Gemini
Element: Fire and Earth

Another creature that holds sway in the Native
American Zodiac is the Deer. Known for their

looks, cunning, and charisma, they can draw all kinds of people to them and grab attention with their captivating demeanor.

As a Deer, you can be quite quixotic and free-spirited – always changing interests from one to another according to your whims. Thus, you are known for knowing a little bit about everything.

This does not make you an expert in the field, of course, but this does mean you make a great conversationalist. While some signs struggle to talk to other people, you are a master of your domain when talking to friends and loved ones.

However, this natural whim also makes you impulsive and too emotionally driven. The moment something else grabs your attention, you tend to leave your post, resulting in work being left behind and things being done haphazardly.

As such, it may be necessary for you to find your life's inner focus to help yourself become more productive.

Woodpecker
June 21 – July 21
Alternate Zodiac Sign: Cancer
Element: Water

The Woodpecker is a protective creature that often tries to make sure that their loved ones are comfortable. In your case, this means that you tend to prioritize other people before your own self to help everything be better for them.

In romance, this makes you a top-tier pick. You are always devoted and willing to do everything in your power – sometimes even throwing people under the bus – if it means that the love of your life feels cherished and important.

Likewise, this also makes you a great friend. You often offer great advice and will use your life skills to help your friends get themselves together. You may even find yourself running errands or doing chores for them to help them out.

You are energetic and always willing to throw yourself between your friends and danger. However, there are times when this protectiveness can become a bit much. If you are not careful, you may compromise too much of your time and end up setting yourself back.

Salmon

July 22 – August 21
Alternate Zodiac Sign: Leo
Element: Fire and Water

If the Woodpecker devotes itself to other
people, the Salmon stands completely by their

own goals. Being a Salmon means constantly craving competition and challenge. Your expectations of yourself and your goals are all equally lofty.

Your ambitious standards invariably allow you to do things that other people might normally not do. For example, at work, you dedicate yourself to pursuing greater pay or getting a promotion by willing to do overtime or go the extra mile.

Consequently, you are willing to sacrifice your social life for the sake of getting your personal objectives done. You may not think about romance or making any new friends if it does not help you advance your own career.

Naturally, this also means that you can sometimes push your agenda ahead of everyone else's – to their dismay. You may end up prioritizing your own concerns over the needs of other people, and as such, you can often destroy your own relationships.

As such, remember that greatness should not come at anyone's expense.

Brown Bear

August 22 – September 21
Alternate Zodiac Sign: Virgo
Element: Water and Earth

An esteemed animal of the Native American zodiac, the Brown Bear is unbelievably patient and sagacious. Everything they say has a natural authority and wit to them, and as such, they are treasured advisors to anyone lucky enough to befriend them.

As a Brown Bear, you have a wealth of experience behind you – be it in career, romance, or friendships. You are perceptive and able to read what other people feel, enough that you can transmit this knowledge to others.

You are intellectually inclined to the core, always willing to read up on history and learn how other people manage their lives. You then end up applying many of these teachings to your own life, making sure that you always have the means to succeed.

Of course, there are things that you can be extremely wary of – sometimes to the point of defensiveness. You often have social barriers and do not share the full weight of your intellect due to your suspicion of other people's motives.

As such, it can be quite difficult, albeit rewarding, to earn your full trust.

Raven

September 22 – October 22
Alternate Zodiac Sign: Libra
Element: Earth and Air

Many animals in the Native American zodiac
are warlike in their approach to life. However,

there is a stark contrast: the Raven is a natural diplomat and a pacifist at heart, always wanting to avoid violence no matter what.

This means that you are naturally measured in your dealings with other people, always careful about what words you might utter. You do your best not to offend other people by always assuming stances that are objective and morally upright.

At work, you are a capable uniter. You look beyond the occasional pettiness of office politics and make sure that everyone is in perfect sync. Whenever there is a conflict, you always find creative ways to defuse the situation. As a result, you usually save the day.

However, because of your own pacifism, you may have difficulty assuming hard stances and making difficult choices. Whenever you are in a dilemma between right and wrong, you may sometimes refuse to condemn evil.

Snake

October 23 – November 22
Alternate Zodiac Sign: Scorpio
Element: Water and Earth

The Snake is pliable and often keeps their plans and motives to themselves. This gives them a mysterious aura that helps them hide when needed.

In your case, this means that you are calculating with your interactions. You do not just aim straight for the goal and go in for the kill. Instead, you keep a keen eye out for any opportunity and seize it only when you know things are going to go extremely well.

You also have an immense knowledge of yourself – you have a clear goal, and you are in touch with your own spiritual nature. This gives you a clarity of mind and a defined purpose that allows you to rise to any occasion where most people would flounder.

In a way, however, this profound knowledge also makes you incredibly difficult to vibe with. Your interests and style of interaction are niche, to the point where people do not often get you. This can make you seem intimidating, but in a good way, because people will think twice about betraying or angering you.

It is easy for you to adapt to change because you simply shed your coat and prepare for the new season.

Owl

November 23 – December 21
Alternate Zodiac Sign: Sagittarius
Element: Earth and Fire

The Owl is the introspective animal in the
Native American zodiac. Full of insight into

the harsh realities of the world, they often stop and pause to think about their very place in the universe as well as the consequences of every action they make.

Being an Owl, you refuse to take things for granted and you do not allow anything to escape your analytical mind. Whether you are trying to solve a problem or thinking about the morality of your actions, you always give it your all when you think.

However, you do not just sit down and think, either. You can let loose when needed. One night, you could be thinking about the world and the meaning of our existence, and the next, you could be drinking outside with your social group.

Of course, it is not all depth and breadth with the Owl. While you do have an affinity for enlightenment, you can also be surprisingly self-indulgent. You can form habits which run contrary to reason, and it can be self-destructive. In such situations, care and caution are your natural allies.

Goose
December 22 – January 19
Alternate Zodiac Sign: Capricorn
Element: Earth and Air

Geese are orderly creatures who embody discipline in everything that they do. When there is something that needs doing, they can shelve their thoughts and follow orders.

This penchant for efficiency and order makes them a highly worthy candidate for the workplace. You are obedient and willing to do what must be done to achieve total victory. Others may be egotistical, but you can see the larger picture.

Additionally, you are also very loving. Since you understand instinctively that love is an essential part of order, you show kindness to the people around you and make friendships zealously.

However, these tendencies also mean that you might have difficulties thriving in a world of discord. If your relationships are not harmonious, you tend to feel lost and unable to figure out what to do.

Obedience can be your primary problem, and only self-sufficiency can cure it.

About the Creators

Janka Latečková is a freelance artist living in the small historic town of Nitra in Slovakia. She has always been fascinated with history (especially ancient era and medieval times) and Slavic and Greek mythology. As a child she was attracted to fantasy books, and later movies. She discovered the world of Tolkien's *Lord of the Rings* and fell in love with the fantasy genre.

Janka was her own art teacher. The artists who influenced her most were Alan Lee, John Howe, Donato Giancola and Todd Lockwood. She has always been drawn to traditional media. She prefers drawing people and animals (fantasy or real) but also enjoys creating fantasy or sci-fi cities and landscapes. Janka likes the roughness, even the mistakes, that come with traditional media.

Janka's art is in private collections and magazines and her illustrations can be found in e-books, books, and comics. Her greatest success is that her art is part of the documents to the extended edition of *The Hobbit - The Battle of Five Armies*.

JS Moore was born in Kingsport, Tennessee but grew up all over the northeastern Tennessee region. While serving in the United States Army as a military police officer in Puerto Rico, Moore was introduced to Hunter S. Thompson and says it was almost like looking into a mirror.

After military service Moore returned to Tennessee where he attended Northeast State Community College and then studied English and history at East Tennessee State University.

His website is: www.understandingapples.com

Nonfiction by JS Moore:
Understanding Apples
Gathering Leaves
Rooting Branches
Mending Wall
Meeting Majesties
Shifting Cairns
Picking Strawberries
The Big Mac Book
Haggard Harry and the Holy Grail
Haggard Harry and the Fisher King
Haggard Harry and the Bountiful Harvest
Haggard Harry and the Infernal Machine
Haggard Harry and the Five Monkeys
The Meeting Place
Funny Business
Pranking Pals

Childrens Books:
Outside Kitty
Harmony on the Farm
Christmas Kitty
Searching Seasons
Best Friend Milou
Wee Willard Tremble
Kingdom of the Dragons

Under the Sun: The Miyamoto Musashi
Story

Random Writings and Poetry:
FIRE GIVER
The Gorgon Remains
The Golden Mean
The Elder Scroll
The Twilight of the Gods

Card decks and Guidebooks:
Catharsis Tarot
The Fantastic Myths and Legends Tarot
The Egyptian Book of the Dead Tarot
The Twilight of the Gods Tarot: The Delphic
Maxims
The Sentient Tarot
The Native American Medicine Tarot

Writing under the Pseudonym Lively Thorne:
Searchers: The Phantom Bookshelf
Searchers: The Divine Web